Souper Jenny GOES VEGAN

ATLANTA'S SOUP DIVA
SHARES HER LOVE OF VEGGIES

JENNIFER LEVISON
PHOTOGRAPHY BY JOEL SILVERMAN
COVER PHOTO BY BREEANNE CLOWDUS

Copyright © 2016 Jennifer Levison

All rights reserved. No part of this book may be reproduced or transmitted in any form or by any means, electronic or mechanical, including photocopying, recording, or by any information storage and retrieval system, without permission in writing from the publisher.

Cover & Book Design: Angela K Aquino
Production Editor & Project Manager: Hope Mirlis
Photography: Joel Silverman, BreeAnne Clowdus, Tom Meyer, Berta Borukhova, Amy Henry
Index: Wendy Allex

ISBN: 978-0-9983781-0-7

Printed and bound in the United States
First printing, 2016

This book is dedicated to the entire Planet Jenny family, who work tirelessly to create the culture and vision of what we do daily.

To my family, including my son, Jonah, who I hope one day will become less picky and actually eat at one of our restaurants!

6   Foreword
8   Introduction
10 The Planet Jenny Family
12 Why Vegan?

14 Soups
26 Salads
42 Veggies
56 Tofu
62 Burgers
68 Juices
84 Smoothies
96 Gluten-free Baking
114 Fun Stuff

122 Special Thanks
124 Index

FOREWORD

The first time I met Jenny was at my café, Bella Cucina, in Atlanta, Georgia. I noticed her strong presence as she sat quietly at the bar counter savoring a bowl of marinated citrus-fennel olives and eating a pressed panini sandwich. Little did I know at the time, she is hardly the quiet type!

Through our love of food, we became fast friends and entrepreneurial allies. Twenty-something years later, we've shared many meals (and cocktails!) brainstorming about our businesses and ways we can share our passion with the world. Conversations of bold and brave ideas turned into daring each other to make our latest aspirations and dreams come true. Planet Jenny, the parent company of Jenny's restaurants, was born out of that bravery. Jenny's desire to feed the world resonates with me and so many others. Food isn't just about what tastes good, it's about food that nourishes and nurtures us – body, mind and spirit. Planet Jenny is about making people feel good, inside and out.

Jenny's vibrant personality positively radiates through her work. Her commitment to community and hospitality is evident in the family of cafés, cooking classes and projects that give back that Jenny continues to create. Whether it's supporting a local fundraising event, making a Sunday supper for twelve, or everyday eating at one of her charming cafés, Jenny is the heartbeat you feel when you experience these lively spaces or events.

If I had to sum up how I see Jenny's work in a few words, it would be:

> "Life tastes better when you're doing good while eating good food with family and friends."

Jenny's commitment to expanding her business to include all kinds of alternative options of eating continues. She's adventurous and willing to learn how she can better serve her community. This cookbook is a perfect example of living that philosophy out loud. And one we all cannot only appreciate, but aspire to live by!

Alisa Barry
Creator,
Bella Cucina Artful Food

Welcome to Souper Jenny Goes Vegan!

OUR FIRST COOKBOOK, *SOUPER JENNY COOKS*, CENTERED AROUND SOUP, WAS PUBLISHED IN 2008. IN 2012, WE SHARED SOME OF OUR FAVORITE SALAD RECIPES IN *SOUPER JENNY DOES SALADS*. NOW, FIVE YEARS LATER, I CAN'T BELIEVE I DIDN'T RUN WHEN IT WAS SUGGESTED THAT A TRILOGY WOULD BE A NICE COLLECTION FOR THE HOME COOK!

Wow. I cannot believe it has been 17 years since I opened my first restaurant, Souper Jenny. With a staff of three and oodles of energy, I can honestly say that my mission has not changed since day one. With four Souper Jenny cafes spread throughout Atlanta, plus continuous educational and community projects, I decided to create the umbrella, Planet Jenny. I see it as something larger than the restaurants and there is a real possibility for growth. Planet Jenny is a community of people striving to feed Atlanta's bodies and souls through our commitment to become a more conscious company from the inside out. The people I have met, the lessons I have learned and the satisfaction I still get today when I see a guest taking a moment for themselves as they nourish their spirit and body with healthy food, has become the center of who I am.

First off, don't let the word "vegan" scare you! This cookbook represents my ideal of how I'd "like" to eat all the time. I love food, just like you and I really can't see myself giving up anything 100%, even if it may increase my lifespan a few years. I can't say I will never again have gluten or dairy or meat, but the truth is, no matter how much I resist, I cannot deny how much better I feel physically and mentally when I avoid them in my diet. There is nothing more delicious than a giant bowl of homemade pasta with butter and fresh cheese and I absolutely intend to have one, but these days, it's a treat and not the norm and my body thanks me for it.

In 2013, I opened a juice bar called Juicy Jenny. Pretty soon after we opened, my good friend, and fellow restauranteur, Michael Patrick suggested we add food to the mix. He was right. There were very few places in Atlanta that were serving a 100% organic, vegan and gluten-free menu and once we started offering lunch, there was no turning back. As I researched and tested recipes, even I was deliciously surprised at how I didn't miss animal protein. It is such an urban myth that there isn't enough protein in plant-based foods and it has become one of my missions to educate anyone who will listen that you don't need to look towards animals to get enough protein in your diet. Did you know that there is 10 grams of protein in one handful of spinach? When I sauté spinach, I probably use four handfuls, just for one serving. That's 40 grams! Research it yourself. You won't believe it.

Juicy Jenny was open for three years before the landlords changed and they tripled our lease. The costs of labor, overhead, and organic ingredients were just not balancing with the price I felt we could charge, and I did not want to lower the quality of what we were producing. Therefore, we decided to close our doors. The experience was extremely informative and I learned some valuable lessons. Organic produce is expensive and still not as much a part of the mainstream as it needs to be. When there is more demand, farmers will produce more and they will become cheaper. I happen to have a pretty high standard when it comes to knowing where my food comes from and I wasn't going to compromise at Juicy Jenny especially with the juice. Sure, non-organics would be cheaper, but who wants to drink pure juice laden with pesticides and GMOs? Not me. I am extremely passionate about good food, good people, and nourishing our community through sitting around the table and sharing an experience. It was my mission to teach our community more about whole foods and how they play a role in our daily health. And so the mission continues in this cookbook.

Souper Jenny Goes Vegan is for anyone that loves to eat and loves to eat well. Looking down at a plate and seeing a gorgeous, colorful rainbow of food, satisfies me to the core. If you have a plate filled with color, you can be sure that you are getting the nutrients your body needs.

This book is written for the home cook and is extremely easy to follow. The recipes are simple and I always encourage mixing and matching ingredients since that is the real joy of creative cooking.

For those of you who don't know me personally, writing down an actual recipe is excruciating! I like to cook by feel, by taste and color. Even when I teach, that is really how I want first time cooks to look at food and cooking, so it's accessible and fun. There are so many ways to experiment and change a single dish and that is what I want people to learn. Plant-based cooking is vibrant – filled with varying textures, tastes and colors. As you explore how to use different vegetables and grains, you will become more comfortable with how you can play with them and try out your own combinations.

As always, feel free to visit me in the cafes or email me with any questions and comments!

Okay, enough preaching. I hope you use this book to get your creative juices flowing. If you are not totally inspired, pour yourself a big glass of wine and enjoy the pictures of my family!

Remember, I am always available for feedback. Feel free to stop by one of the restaurants. If you're not in Atlanta, email me at souperjenny@aol.com.

Jenny

Indispensable...

THAT'S THE ONLY WORD THAT COMES TO MIND WHEN I THINK ABOUT THE 40+ INCREDIBLE PEOPLE THAT MAKE THE PLANET JENNY BUSINESSES RUN EFFICIENTLY AND THOUGHTFULLY. I USE THE TERM, "PLANET JENNY" SINCE WE'RE NOW MORE THAN JUST "SOUPER JENNY" AND HAVE EXCITING PLANS ON THE HORIZON.

In 1999, I opened my very first Souper Jenny cafe with three employees and myself. I showed up every morning at 5 AM to make the food. My friends Collin Lines, Meg McGarry and Sarah Reidy joined me at 9 AM and together we prepped, served and cleaned until 5 PM. It was an exciting and exhausting time and I think back and am honored that Collin, Meg and Sarah were there for support during those early days. They were among the first to really get the vision of encouraging our guests to take a moment, sit down and eat real food without outside interruption.

Just to give you a little backstory, the original Souper Jenny on East Andrews Drive was the first and only restaurant for 10 years. I never even thought about opening anything else. Out of nowhere, this adorable house around the corner was for rent and I felt inspired to open Cafe Jonah and The Magical Attic in 2011. Named after my son, Jonah, we created a delightful coffee shop and eatery downstairs and featured a metaphysical store upstairs. In the warm months we had picnic dinners and movie nights in the garden out back.

In 2014, we opened Juicy Jenny – Atlanta's first completely gluten-free and vegan organic juice bar and cafe. The tiny shop, a few stores away from the original Souper Jenny, was inspired by my southern California youth and the fresh food available on the West coast. The amazing amount of research I did and experience I gained got me excited to write this book.

Unfortunately the property where Cafe Jonah sat was sold forcing us to close in February of 2016. Just a few short months later Juicy Jenny's lease ended and that property was sold, so we were forced to shut our doors. I will never regret these two adventures. I get numerous requests for them to re-open and you never know, they might show up again!

That being said, we opened the second Souper Jenny in Decatur and Souper Jenny Westside in 2014. Souper Jenny Brookhaven opened in 2015. And our original Buckhead location moved to the gorgeous and newly renovated Atlanta History Center in May of 2016.

It has been quite a ride since that first day in 1999, but the one constant is my hardworking, loyal staff that shows the rest of Atlanta that there is still a place where you can expect incredible service and hospitality.

Some fantastic changes have happened over the past decade...

> Six years ago, Jessica Hanners became our Executive Chef – which means I don't have to go to work at 5 AM anymore! If you want to read an entire love letter to Jessica, check out our salad book! She and I share the same passion about food and service and I can't imagine anyone else running our kitchens as seamlessly as she does.

> I was introduced to Eric Miller by his fabulous wife, Rachel, one of our shining star servers. Eric started in the front of house, but we quickly realized he was a 'jack of all trades' and before he even knew it, we created a CFO position that was a perfect fit for him. I love Eric because he is way more responsible than I am and will keep me out of jail! I like to cook and if it were up to me I'd give everything away for free. Eric is in charge of everything financial and he can never leave! Do you hear that, Eric?

> When you have more than one restaurant, management becomes extremely important. You need someone that has finesse and grace to deal with every possible situation, as well as every front of house employee and their needs. It is not an easy task. I met Keith Yeager in 2012 when he repeatedly stopped by Cafe Jonah to let me know that he loved our company and mission and would love to be involved. I was so busy that I didn't take him seriously until maybe the fourth visit when a light bulb went off. Keith was the perfect missing piece of our puzzle. He is now the General Manager of Operations for all four restaurants.

Even after all of these years, our kitchens are still run by the fierce Perez/Maldonado family. I have never met a group of people that could stand on their feet for so many hours, take such pride in their food and all the while laugh and have a good time. I literally have almost all my original culinary crew (including Papa Rigo, who has been with me almost from the beginning and currently heads up the kitchen in Decatur) plus the additions of Izzie running our Buckhead kitchen like he's been doing it for years, Lidia, our Chef in Brookhaven who can pretty much cook circles around anyone and works in the space the size of a tea cup and Julio, Izzie's brother who has moved up through the years to be the Chef at our Westside location. The rest of the kitchen staff is a team of super heroes – Irene, Anna, Suzy, Andres, Rosie, Moy, Therese, Lulu, Jessica, Christian. Rockstars. Each and every one of you.

EVERYONE THAT WORKS AT ONE OF OUR RESTAURANTS NOT ONLY KNOWS, BUT LIVES OUR MISSION STATEMENT.

Planet Jenny is a collection of community cafes striving to nourish your body, mind and spirit. We serve fabulously fresh food prepared with love by passionate people who care about you and how you move through your day. We want each guest to leave our cafes saying, "I love this place, I love the way I feel when I'm here and I can't wait to come back!"

We want our guests to feel like they are a guest in our home – or my home! At the time of this printing, we have four Souper Jenny cafes around Atlanta and our servers are the key to their experience. You will still find Merrideth Ziesse, with her infectious laugh and free hugs, Ivan Perez who has practically grown up in our kitchen, Marshall Smith, a customer favorite because he will bend over backwards to please a guest, as well as a bevy of super friendly, loving hard working individuals that treat their co-workers and their customers like family.

Let us know how we're doing!

SOUPER JENNY GOES VEGAN

Veganism is the new hot topic in the culinary world. Here's why...

ACTUALLY, PLANT-BASED DIETS HAVE BEEN AROUND SINCE THE BEGINNING OF TIME, BUT IT SEEMS THAT EVERYONE ASSOCIATES VEGANISM WITH THE HIPPIE-DIPPIE, CRUNCHY GRANOLA GROUP OF FOLKS FROM THE 1970s. WELL, WE SHOULD LISTEN TO THEM!

Veganism is the practice of eating a diet without any animal proteins or dairy. This includes meat, poultry, fish, eggs, milk and cheese. Some vegans also abstain from honey since it comes from bees, and don't wear clothes or shoes made of animal hides or leather.

Let me say from the start that I am not vegan. I'm certainly not asking you to completely change your diet to not include animal proteins and dairy. What I am asking is for you to look through these delicious recipes and realize how tasty and nutritious food can be without them. In fact, you won't even miss them. I can promise you that the more whole foods you put into your daily diet including vegetables, nuts, fruits and gluten-free grains, the better you will feel. You will be amazed. I love discovering a new, stinky cheese and pairing it with artisan bread and a good glass of red, but I have changed my habits. Those menu items are now a treat instead of a regular indulgence and I can tell the difference – in my energy, in my clarity, in my entire physical being. There is no denying how I feel when I eat mostly plant-based foods.

A lot of people refer to many plant-based foods as "superfoods." I actually love this term, because we all don't seem to realize how easy it is to get real nutrition from something so simple. Why is kale a super food? Because it's packed with phytonutrients such as glucosinolates and flavonoids. That may be too scientific for most, but thanks to its broad nutritional profile, kale is thought to help fight cardiovascular disease, asthma, and rheumatoid arthritis; to prevent several types of cancer, pre-mature aging of the skin; and to promote the health of the urinary tract. On top of that, ounce for ounce, kale has more iron than beef!

Throughout this book you will find side notes when I feel you should know about a particular "superfood." Otherwise, you can stick to the golden rule that the less ingredients on the package, the better. Grocery stores are also amazing these days. I can find specialty items found in the ingredient lists like maca and gogi berries at the local big-name grocery stores.

I hope you will dig in to this book and also explore your own ideas for each recipe listed. There are so many possibilities for each recipe and my hope is that you will start to experiment and create your own. As always, reach out if you have a question or a comment, and enjoy how you feel as you eat your way to a healthier you!

The more whole foods you put into your diet, the better you will feel.

Soups

Quinoa and Fava Bean Chili

Wild Mushroom Potage

Thai Noodle Bowl

Vegan "Chicken" Tortilla Soup

Creamy Cauliflower Soup

Jenny's Gypsy Soup

SOUPS

Quinoa & Fava Bean Chili

SERVES 8

Get your protein on with this gluten-free and vegan chili!

2 tablespoons extra virgin olive oil
1 large sweet yellow onion or red onion, peeled and diced
2 cloves garlic, peeled and crushed
2 teaspoons cumin powder
1 large zucchini, ends trimmed, cut into chunks
1 large yellow squash, ends trimmed, cut into chunks
1 red pepper, 1 yellow pepper and 1 orange or green pepper, seeded and cut into small chunks
1 tablespoon dark chili powder
1 28-ounce can of chopped tomatoes
1 big handful of fresh spinach, chopped
1 12-ounce can fava beans or 1 1/2 cups frozen fava (or lima) beans
1 12-ounce can of chili beans, do not drain liquid
1 cup fresh or frozen corn kernels
3 cups quinoa, cooked (see page 36 for how to cook quinoa)
1 bunch cilantro, chopped (cut off the bottom two inches of stems)
salt & pepper to taste

In a heavy soup pot, heat olive oil. Sauté onions and garlic at medium heat for a couple of minutes. Add cumin and stir completely. Add zucchini, squash and peppers and sauté until soft - about 10 minutes. Add chili powder and stir for a few minutes to coat veggies. Add tomatoes and spinach and let veggies stew in the tomatoes for about 5 to 10 minutes on low heat, stirring frequently. Add all beans, corn and quinoa and simmer on low for 15 minutes. Add cilantro and salt and pepper to taste.

Wild Mushroom Potage

3 tablespoons extra virgin olive oil
1 large sweet yellow onion, peeled and diced
4 cloves garlic, peeled and crushed
12 ounces shitake mushrooms, cleaned and sliced
12 ounces baby portobello mushrooms, cleaned and sliced
12 ounces white button mushrooms, cleaned and sliced
12 ounces oyster mushrooms, cleaned and sliced
2 cups dry sherry
4 quarts vegetable broth
8 ounces frozen, chopped spinach or 1 pound fresh, baby spinach, chopped
4 ounces coconut milk

Heat large soup pot and add olive oil to heat. Sauté the onion and garlic on medium to low heat for about 3 minutes until soft. Add all of the mushrooms and coat with the olive oil, onion and garlic mixture. Sauté until mushroom mixture is soft. Add sherry and simmer 3 to 5 minutes. Add vegetable stock and spinach and turn up heat to boil. Once it boils, reduce heat and simmer for 30 minutes. Add coconut milk and simmer another 5 minutes. I like to take a hand blender and pulse the soup a few times leaving it slightly chunky.

SERVES 8

There is nothing more satisfying during those first hints of fall than a piping hot bowl of mushroom soup laced with dry sherry. It's even better when you take out the guilt of cream and butter!

SUPERFOOD NOTE:
1/4 CUP OF SHITAKE MUSHROOMS GIVE YOU AS MUCH VITAMIN D AS A GLASS OF MILK!

SOUPS

Thai Noodle Bowl

1 tablespoon sesame oil
2 tablespoons extra virgin olive oil
1 medium onion, peeled and diced
4 cloves garlic, minced
1 large finger ginger, peeled and minced
1 stalk lemongrass, outer leaves removed, only use white part and slice very thin
12 ounces shitake mushrooms, cleaned and sliced thin
3 tablespoons green or red curry paste
4 quarts vegetable stock or miso broth
1 bunch fresh spinach, cleaned, stems removed
1 cake firm tofu, drained and cut into small cubes
1 18-ounce package rice noodles or buckwheat soba
1/2 cup cilantro, chopped
1/2 cup roasted peanuts, crushes
1/2 cup scallions, sliced thin

SERVES 8

Heat your soup pot. On medium low heat add both oils. Sauté onion, garlic, ginger and lemongrass a few minutes until soft. Don't brown. Add shitake mushrooms and sauté until soft. Add chili paste and stir completely. Add broth and spinach and bring to a boil. Lower heat and add tofu. Simmer on low for 15 minutes and then add rice noodles. Cook about 3 minutes. Top with cilantro, crushed peanuts and scallions!

Vegan "Chicken" Tortilla Soup

SERVES 8

3 tablespoons extra virgin olive oil
1 large yellow onion, peeled and chopped
1 red pepper, one green pepper and one yellow pepper, seeded and chopped
1 tablespoon dark chili powder
2 cups fresh or frozen corn kernels
1 28-ounce can chopped tomatoes
4 quarts vegetable broth
2 cups baked tempeh, cut into small cubes
3 cups corn tortilla chips
2 cups vegan cheddar cheese (I like the Daya brand!)
1/2 cup cilantro, chopped

Heat your soup pot and then add olive oil. Add the onions and peppers and sauté on medium heat until soft - about 10 minutes. Add the chili powder and stir completely. Add the corn, tomato, vegetable broth, tempeh and bring to a boil. Lower heat and simmer for 30 minutes. Crush up tortilla chips, add to soup and simmer 5 more minutes. Turn off heat and stir in cheese and cilantro and serve!

SOUPS

Starting with a good olive oil is key!

Creamy Cauliflower Soup

SERVES 6 TO 8

1/2 cup raw cashews
1 medium red onion, diced
2 bell peppers, cleaned and chopped
2 tablespoon extra virgin olive oil
3 stalks celery, chopped
2 carrots, chopped
2 cloves garlic, minced
1 1/2 heads of cauliflower, core removed and chopped
8 cups vegetable broth
1 teaspoon salt (more or less to taste)
freshly ground black pepper
a couple sprigs fresh thyme, to taste

Preheat oven to 400°F.

Place cashews in a bowl and cover with warm water. Set aside.

Place red onion and bell pepper on a baking sheet. Add oil and toss to coat. Bake for 20 to 25 minutes, stirring halfway, or until veggies are golden.

Heat a soup pot or dutch oven over medium heat and add a drizzle of olive oil. Once hot, add carrots and celery. Sauté for 5 minutes. Add garlic and cauliflower and sauté for another 5 minutes. Add roasted vegetables, thyme, and vegetable broth. Bring to a boil and then reduce heat to low and simmer (covered) for about 20 minutes or until cauliflower is tender.

Ladle a couple cups of soup into a high-speed blender. Add cashews and blend (careful, it will be hot) until completely smooth. Blend the rest of the soup in batches until smooth and creamy.

Season with salt, pepper, and thyme to taste.

Jenny's Gypsy Soup

SERVES 8

2 carrots, peeled and cut into carrot coins
1/2 a bunch of celery, chopped including leaves
1 onion - yellow, red, leeks...anything, peeled and chopped
1 squash, chopped
1 zucchini, chopped
a handful of okra, tops removed and chopped
1 28-ounce can chopped tomatoes
1 handful spinach (this was actually leftover salad from the night before with nuts and cranberries!)
6 ounces sliced mushrooms
8 ounces frozen or canned fava beans
8 ounces canned chickpeas, drained
1 bunch swiss chard, ribs removed and chopped
4 quarts vegetable broth
1 tablespoon fresh thyme
2 tablespoons parsley, chopped

Throw everything except the parsley into a large soup pot. If the vegetable broth is not at least 2 inches above the veggies, add more. Bring to a boil. Lower heat and simmer for 45 minutes.

(If you are not vegan, throw in chicken or turkey meatballs at the end! Shhhhhhhh!)

Add parsley and serve!

Inspired by one of my first and favorites, The Moosewood Cookbook. I loved reading this wonderful cookbook and being inspired that anything can be turned into a delicious pot of soup! This was an evening of cleaning out the fridge and I challenge you to do the same! You can mix and match your vegetables according to what's in there and I often find myself adding a wilted bunch of lettuce!
And no oil at all here...
Do it!

SOUPS

Salads

Raw Kale & Swiss Chard Slaw with Golden Raisins, Dates, Toasted Almonds & Fresh Herb Dressing

Kale Caesar with Cherry Tomato, Cucumber & Mock Parmesan

Raw Collard, Apple, Sun Dried Figs, Candied Ginger with Apple Cider Vinaigrette

Roasted Golden Beets, Cauliflower & Apples with Honey Dijon Dressing

Raw Six Vegetable Spiralized Salad with Green Tahini Dressing

Jeweled Quinoa with Sautéed Greens, Portobello Mushrooms & Sautéed Tamari Tofu

Golden Quinoa with Grilled Stone Fruit, Butter Beans & Spring Onions with Fresh Lemon Dressing

Red Quinoa, Fresh Corn, Blistered Tomatoes & Avocado

SALADS

Raw Kale & Swiss Chard Slaw
with Golden Raisins, Dates, Toasted Almonds & Fresh Herb Dressing

SERVES 4 TO 6

For the dressing:
1/4 cup red wine vinegar
1/4 cup parsley, chopped
1/4 cup dill, chopped
1 tablespoon dijon mustard
1 garlic clove, pressed
3/4 cup extra virgin olive oil
salt & pepper to taste

In a mixing bowl, combine garlic, herbs, vinegar and mustard. Slowly drizzle in oil until combined. Salt and pepper to taste.

For the salad:
2 bunches of kale, any kind, ribs removed and julienned
2 bunches of swiss chard, ribs removed and julienned
1/2 head napa or green cabbage, core removed and julienned
1 cup golden raisins
1/2 cup pitted dates, rough chopped
1/2 cup fresh basil, sliced thin
1/2 cup almonds, sliced, toasted

In a large bowl mix all ingredients together. Add dressing sparingly until dressed to the amount you like!

SUPERFOOD NOTE:
DARK LEAFY GREENS ARE LOW CALORIE AND FILLED WITH ANTIOXIDANTS AND TONS OF VITAMINS!

Kale Caesar
with Cherry Tomato, Cucumber & Mock Parmesan

For the dressing:
1/2 cup cashews, soaked overnight and rinsed well
1/3 cup + 1 tablespoon water
1 teaspoon extra virgin olive oil
1/2 lemon, juiced
1 teaspoon Dijon mustard
1 1/2 tablespoons minced capers
2 garlic cloves
1 teaspoon tamari
1 tablespoon nutritional yeast
salt & pepper to taste

Puree cashews and 1/3 cup water in blender until smooth. Add all other ingredients. Thin with additional water, as needed.

For the mock parmesan:
1/3 cup cashews, soaked overnight and rinsed well
2 tablespoons hemp seeds
2 garlic cloves, peeled
1 tablespoon nutritional yeast
1 tablespoon extra virgin olive oil

Pulse first 4 items in food processor and slowly add oil. Mixture should look crumbly!

For the salad:
2 heads kale, ribs removed and roughly chopped
1 pint cherry tomatoes, cut in half
1 large cucumber, washed and sliced

In a mixing bowl, massage your kale with your hands for a few minutes to break down the kale. Add tomatoes and cucumber. Add desired amount of dressing and mock parmesan and toss until leaves are coated!

SERVES 4

I am a crazy caesar salad fan, but was always looking for something a little healthier, without losing that delicious caesar taste. This dressing is easy to make and the mock parmesan is optional, but adds the cheesiness I love!

SUPERFOOD NOTE:
NUTRITIONAL YEAST IS KNOWN FOR ITS CHEESY FLAVOR. IT'S FILLED WITH PROTEIN AND FIBER AND ONE OF THE ONLY VEGAN SOURCES OF VITAMIN B12!

SALADS

Raw Collard, Apple, Sun Dried Figs & Candied Ginger
with Apple Cider Vinaigrette

SERVES 4

1 large bunch of collards, middle ribs removed and julienned
2 crunchy apples, core removed, sliced thin or in small chunks
 and tossed with 2 tablespoons of fresh lemon juice
1 cup sun dried figs, stem removed and chopped into small pieces
1/4 cup candied ginger, sliced as thin as possible

In a mixing bowl, massage collards with hands for a few minutes. Add apples, figs and ginger. Toss lightly with dressing.

For the vinaigrette:
2 cloves garlic, peeled and put through garlic press
1 tablespoon Dijon mustard
1/4 cup raw apple cider vinegar
2 tablespoons fresh lemon juice
1 tablespoon maple syrup or agave
1/3 cup extra virgin olive oil
salt & pepper to taste

In mixing bowl whisk first five ingredients together and slowly drizzle in oil. Add salt and pepper to taste.

Roasted Golden Beets, Cauliflower & Apples
with Honey Dijon Dressing

SERVES 4

I love this salad because it's made with three of my favorite things! Beets, cauliflower and apples! It's also delicious served hot, cold or room temperature!

2 medium golden beets, scrubbed and beet greens removed
2 medium crunchy apples, cored and cut into chunks
1 head of cauliflower, cored and cut into pieces
4 tablespoons extra virgin olive oil
1/2 cup pistachios, toasted
1/2 cup flat leaf parsley, chopped

Heat oven to 400°F. Wrap beets loosely in foil and roast for 1 hour. They are ready when you can easily put a knife through them. Toss the cauliflower and apples together with olive oil and spread on a baking sheet. Roast in the oven for the last 15 minutes that the beets are cooking. Toast the pistachios on a cookie sheet in the oven the last 5 minutes that the beets and cauliflower cook.

Remove everything from the oven. Let beets cool a bit and then with kitchen gloves or paper towels, remove skin from beets. Cut into chunks about the same size as your cauliflower and apples.

Toss with Honey Dijon Dressing and the parsley. Salt and pepper to taste.

For the dressing:
1/3 cup honey
2 tablespoons Dijon mustard
1 tablespoon fresh lemon juice
1/2 cup extra virgin olive oil

Whisk all ingredients together.

SALADS

SALADS

Raw Six Vegetable Spiralized Salad
with Green Tahini Dressing

SERVES 4 AS A SIDE OR TWO AS A MAIN DISH

2 medium zucchini, ends trimmed
1 medium yellow squash, ends trimmed
1 large watermelon radish, ends trimmed and peeled
3 carrots, peeled, ends trimmed and cut in half
1 large red beet, peeled, ends trimmed
1 large golden beet, peeled and ends trimmed

Spiralize each vegetable separately and then toss together. Add small amount of tahini dressing. The salad should not be overdressed, so add sparingly.

For the dressing:
2 cloves garlic, peeled
1 bunch watercress, thick stems trimmed
1 cup fresh mint leaves
1 cup flat leaf parsley, stems removed
1 cup tahini
1/2 cup fresh lemon juice

Purée everything in food processor until smooth.

SALADS

Jeweled Quinoa
with Sautéed Greens, Portobello Mushrooms & Sautéed Tamari Tofu

SERVES 6 TO 8

4 cups vegetable broth
2 cups golden or red quinoa, rinsed
2 tablespoons extra virgin olive oil
1 cake extra firm tofu, water drained, cut in half lengthwise and then into small cubes
2 cloves garlic, peeled and sliced thin
4 large portobello mushroom caps, wiped clean, stem removed, chopped into small cubes
2 cups fresh baby spinach
1 bunch swiss chard, ribs removed, julienned
1 bunch kale, ribs removed, julienned
2 tablespoons tamari
2 tablespoons scallions, chopped
salt & pepper to taste

In a sauce pan, bring the broth and quinoa to a boil. Lower heat and simmer covered for 15 minutes. Turn heat off and remove from stove.

In a large sauté pan, heat 1 tablespoon of olive oil. Add tofu and tamari and sauté until browned on each side. With tongs remove tofu. Add remaining tablespoon of olive oil to sauté pan. Add garlic and sauté until soft. Add portobello mushrooms and sauté about 5 minutes until soft. Add all greens except scallion and cover to wilt. Remove everything from the heat.

Fluff the quinoa with a fork. In a mixing bowl, toss all the ingredients together. Add scallions. Season with salt and pepper.

SALADS

SALADS

I love the bite of spring onions combined with the sweetness of summer fruit!

Golden Quinoa
with Grilled Stone Fruit, Butter Beans, Spring Onions & Fresh Lemon Dressing

SERVES 6 TO 8

6 cups vegetable broth
2 cups golden quinoa, rinsed
3 peaches or plums, cut in half, pit removed
2 teaspoons extra virgin olive oil
2 cups frozen butter beans
2 tablespoons spring onions, chopped
2 tablespoons parsley, chopped
1/2 cup sun dried cranberries
salt & pepper to taste

In a sauce pan, bring 4 cups broth and quinoa to a boil. Lower heat and simmer covered for 15 minutes. Turn heat off and remove from stove.

Heat grill. Brush the cut side of peaches with oil and place face down on grill. Grill for 2 minutes on each side and remove. Cut peaches into small pieces.

Bring the remaining 2 cups of broth to a boil. Add butter beans and lower heat. Simmer 20 minutes or until beans are tender and drain.

Fluff quinoa with a fork.

In a mixing bowl, toss quinoa with butter beans, peaches, scallions, parsley, cranberries and the lemon dressing. Season to taste.

For the dressing:
3 tablespoons fresh lemon juice
1 teaspoon sea salt
1 clove garlic, minced
1/2 cup extra virgin olive oil

In a mixing bowl, combine lemon, salt and garlic. Slowly whisk in oil until combined.

Red Quinoa, Fresh Corn, Blistered Tomatoes & Avocado

SERVES 6 TO 8

4 cups vegetable broth
2 cups golden quinoa, rinsed
1 pint cherry tomatoes
1 pint baby sun gold or yellow tomatoes
2 tablespoons extra virgin olive oil
3 ears of corn, shucked and removed from cob
2 avocados, pitted, removed from skin and cut into small pieces
1 tablespoon red wine vinegar
1 tablespoon fresh chives, minced
salt & pepper to taste

Heat oven to 400°F.

In a sauce pan, bring broth and quinoa to a boil. Lower heat and simmer, covered for 15 minutes. Turn heat off and remove from stove.

Toss all tomatoes with olive oil and roast on a baking sheet for 15 minutes or until tomatoes look like they are about to burst. Remove from oven and toss with the vinegar.

In a mixing bowl toss quinoa, tomato mixture, corn, avocado and chives. Salt and pepper to taste.

SALADS

Veggies

Roasted Rainbow

Roasted Sweet & Spicy Sweet Potatoes with Romesco Sauce

Braised Turnips with Miso

Zucchini Spaghetti with the Most Delicious Vegan Pesto

Red & Yellow Peppers Stuffed with Millet Salad

Juicy Jenny Collard Wraps

My Favorite Vegetable Tacos with Tomatillos & Pico De Gallo

Spaghetti Squash with Chunky Vegetable Marinara

VEGGIES

Roasted Rainbow

SERVES 4

Colorful, simple and delicious. Try to cut everything around the same size and you can certainly change up the veggies to include your favorites! Better yet, throw leftovers in a soup or chop smaller and add to your bean burgers!

2 cups carrots, peeled and chopped small
2 cups Brussels sprouts, cleaned, ends removed and cut in half
1 yellow pepper, cleaned, seeds removed and chopped
1 red pepper, cleaned, seeds removed and chopped
1 large red onion, peeled and chopped
2 cups butternut squash, peeled, pulp removed and chopped
3 tablespoons extra virgin olive oil
2 tablespoons fresh rosemary, chopped fine
2 tablespoons balsamic or red wine vinegar
salt & pepper to taste

Preheat oven to 400°F.

In a large mixing bowl, toss the first 8 ingredients together and spread on a baking sheet.

Roast for 15 minutes and then stir veggies, moving them around. Roast another 10 minutes until they look crispy on the outside.

When you remove from oven, drizzle with the vinegar and add salt and pepper to taste.

Roasted Sweet & Spicy Sweet Potatoes
with Romesco Sauce

2 medium sweet potatoes, scrubbed and cut into wedges
 (like big french fries)
3 tablespoons extra virgin olive oil
2 tablespoons brown sugar
2 teaspoons chili powder
1/2 teaspoon cayenne pepper

Preheat oven to 400°F. In a mixing bowl toss potatoes with olive oil, brown sugar, chili powder and cayenne until coated. Roast on a cookie sheet for 15 minutes and then turn over and roast another 15 minutes. Serve potatoes with Romesco dipping sauce.

For the sauce:
1/4 cup raw slivered almonds
1 clove garlic, peeled
2 roasted red peppers, homemade or jarred
1 tablespoon extra virgin olive oil
1 tablespoon red wine vinegar
1 teaspoon paprika
Maldon sea salt or kosher salt

In food processor or blender, puree everything until smooth.

SERVES 4

This is an easy and quick nutritious snack or side dish. I like to leave the skin on my potatoes for a boost of nutrition, but feel free to peel, if you prefer!

Braised Turnips with Miso

SERVES 4

2 tablespoons extra virgin olive oil
2 pounds baby turnips, scrubbed, ends removed and quartered
1 cup vegetable broth
1/2 cup miso paste
1 tablespoon agave

In a sauté pan, heat the olive oil and sauté turnips on medium low heat until they start to brown. Add vegetable broth, lower heat and cover. Simmer for 15 minutes. Add miso and agave, stir to fully coat turnips. Simmer another 15 minutes, covered and add a little broth, if necessary. Turnips should be glossy and tender!

Zucchini Spaghetti
with the Most Delicious Vegan Pesto

5 medium sized zucchini, ends cut

Spiralize zucchini and toss with a small amount of pesto, add more as you desire.

For the pesto:
1/2 cup extra virgin olive oil
1 lemon, juiced
4 garlic cloves, peeled
3 tablespoons nutritional yeast
1 cup pine nuts, toasted for 10 minutes at 350°F
2 cups basil leaves, stems off
salt & pepper to taste

Combine all ingredients in food processor until smooth and creamy.
Salt and pepper to taste.

**SERVES 4 AS A SIDE DISH
OR 2 AS A MAIN DISH**

You can spiralize almost any veggie!

VEGGIES

VEGGIES

Red & Yellow Peppers Stuffed with Millet Salad

SERVES 4

Millet is another delicious, underutilized gluten-free grain which also happens to be an alkaline food. The body needs to maintain a proper balance of neutral, acidic and alkaline foods for optimum health. Alkaline foods such as vegetables, fruits and grains can help! Millet is mild in taste and can be flavored in many ways, just like rice. This dish is filling and one of my favorite dinners served with a green salad!

1 tablespoon extra virgin olive oil
2 yellow onions, peeled and chopped
4 garlic cloves, minced
2 cups chopped tomatoes (canned)
1 cup dry millet
2 cups vegetable broth
2 cups fresh spinach, chopped
1/2 cup parsley, chopped
1 cup golden raisins
1 cup pine nuts, toasted
2 red and 2 yellow peppers, tops and seeds removed
salt & pepper to taste

Make a quick tomato sauce by heating a sauce pan and adding 1 tablespoon of oil. Sauté 1 onion and 2 cloves garlic 4 to 5 minutes until soft. Add tomatoes and combine. Lower heat and simmer 20 minutes. Salt and pepper to taste.

Preheat oven to 350°F.

In another sauce pan combine millet, vegetable broth, the other onion and the other 2 garlic cloves. Bring to a boil and then lower heat and simmer for 15 minutes. Remove from stove and let sit covered for 15 minutes. Fluff millet with fork and then combine in a mixing bowl with chopped spinach, parsley, raisins and pine nuts.

Stuff peppers with millet mixture and sit up right in a baking dish. Bake for 20 to 25 minutes uncovered. Remove and top with tomato sauce!

Juicy Jenny Collard Wraps

8 collard leaves, ribs removed
2 cups of the Best Hummus I've Ever Had (recipe on page 122)
1 medium cucumber, peeled and sliced thin
2 carrots, shredded
1 red pepper, seeded and julienned
1 ripe avocado, pitted and sliced
1 cup radish or alfalfa sprouts

First, you need a big bowl of hot water. Lay out a clean cloth on the counter. Put the collard leaves in hot water for about 30 seconds and then remove and lay them on the cloth to dry off water and then flip over to dry the other side. Take two leaves and overlap them a bit. Divide hummus equally and spread down the middle of the collards. Next layer avocado, peppers, cucumber, carrots then sprouts. Fold each side in and then fold the side closest to you away from you. Roll tightly like a burrito. Repeat.

MAKES 4

This was a fantastic and popular sandwich alternative at Juicy Jenny. I am always on the hunt for a tasty sandwich without the bread. Prepared correctly, collards will do the trick!

My Favorite Vegetable Tacos
with Tomatillos & Pico De Gallo

SERVES 4

I'm a Mexican food fanatic, but I've been trying to cut down on my trips to my favorite Mexican joint because the chips and queso taunt me until I give in! When I take the time to make these antioxidant-filled tacos, they do the trick and I don't even miss the cheese!

1 red pepper, seeds out and cut into strips
1 yellow pepper, seeds out and cut into strips
1 large portobello mushroom, wiped clean and cut into thin strips
1 zucchini, cleaned, ends removed and cut in batons
1 cup cherry tomatoes, cut in half
4 tomatillos, paper shell taken off and cut into quarters
3 tablespoons extra virgin olive oil
a dash of white wine vinegar
4 Roma tomatoes, cut into small dice
1 small yellow onion, peeled, diced small
1/2 cup cilantro, chopped
1/2 jalapeño, seeds removed, diced small
1/2 fresh lime
1 avocado, seeds removed, mashed and tossed with a little lime
salt & pepper to taste
8 corn tortillas or 8 romaine lettuce leaves

Preheat oven to 400°F. In a mixing bowl toss the first 6 ingredients with the olive oil. Spread on a baking sheet and roast 20 to 25 minutes until veggies look nice and roasted. Remove and add salt and pepper to taste and a dash of white wine vinegar.

Make pico de gallo by combining chopped tomatoes, onion, cilantro, jalapeño and lime juice. Salt and pepper to taste.

Divide veggies into your tortillas or lettuce leaves and top with fresh pico de gallo and avocado.

Spaghetti Squash
with Summer or Winter Marinara

SERVES 4 TO 6

First prepare the spaghetti squash...

Preheat oven to 375°F.

Cut 2 small to medium spaghetti squash down the middle lengthwise. Clean out seeds from the middle. Put cut sides down on a baking sheet and bake for 35 to 45 minutes. You will know that the squash is done when you can take a fork and scoop out the middle creating strands like pasta.

Spoon either sauce over spaghetti squash.

Spaghetti squash is one of my favorite pasta alternatives. It's delicious, easy to make and holds up great with a sauce. I am happy to eat this for dinner any night of the week. Here is a summer sauce when tomatoes are at their peak and a winter sauce when a good canned tomato is a great substitute.

Summer Marinara

2 tablespoons extra virgin olive oil
1 large sweet onion, peeled and chopped
4 large garlic cloves, minced
5 large tomatoes, seeded and diced (about 3 cups)
1/4 cup fresh basil leaves, minced
1/2 cup oil-packed sun-dried tomatoes (about 10)
2 teaspoons fresh oregano
1 teaspoon teaspoon sea salt, more to taste
freshly ground black pepper, to taste
red pepper flakes, to taste (optional)

In a sauté pan, heat olive oil. Sauté onion and garlic on low heat until onions are soft. Add tomatoes including juice, sun-dried tomatoes, oregano, basil and salt and simmer on low until sauce begins to reduce and thicken. Cook and stir often for about 20 minutes. Add a bit of red pepper flakes and fresh ground pepper to taste.

Winter Marinara

2 tablespoons extra virgin olive oil
1 large sweet onion, peeled and chopped
4 large garlic cloves, peeled and minced
1 tablespoon fresh rosemary, off stem, chopped
2 28-ounce cans Italian chopped tomatoes
  (I like Cento brand)
2 teaspoons fresh oregano
salt & pepper to taste

In sauté pan, heat olive oil. Sauté onion and garlic until soft. Add rosemary, tomatoes, oregano and a pinch of salt. Simmer on low for 30 minutes. Taste and season, if needed.

Tofu

There are a lot of mixed feelings about tofu! Is it bad for you, good for you? Is it genetically modified? I have always been a tofu fan because there are so many ways to season this relatively bland plant protein. It's still easy to find GMO-free varieties. Stick to Eden, Nasoya or Wildwood and you'll be golden. I eat my tofu in moderation and love it on top of a salad or hearty grain, if I am having a meat craving but don't want to eat meat. All three of these recipes are designed to satisfy the pickiest eaters on the planet. My son, Jonah, will even give these a go!

Grilled Sengalese Tofu with Peanuts, Ginger & Curry

Roasted Balsamic Tofu with Gremolata & Cherry Tomatoes

Roasted Poblano Peppers Stuffed with Smoked Tofu

TOFU

Grilled Sengalese Tofu
with Peanuts, Ginger & Curry

SERVES 2 TO 4

1 12- to 14-ounce cake of extra firm tofu
2 tablespoons of your favorite sweet chili sauce (my fav is Mae Ploy!)
1 tablespoon creamy peanut butter
1 tablespoon fresh ginger, grated
1 teaspoon curry powder
1/2 cup roasted peanuts, cashews or your favorite toasted nut

Drain tofu and put it on a plate lined with paper towels and cover with a cloth and heavy can for 20 minutes and then slice tofu into quarter inch slices.

Mix remaining ingredients together and marinate tofu for 30 minutes.

Turn grill on medium heat and grill tofu for two minutes on each side. When you remove tofu from grill, baste with remaining sauce.

Roasted Balsamic Tofu
with Gremolata & Cherry Tomatoes

1 12- to 14-ounce cake of extra firm tofu, drained
3 tablespoons balsamic (or your favorite fruit vinegar)
1 clove garlic, crushed + 1 garlic clove, minced
salt & pepper to taste
1 pint cherry tomatoes, washed, stems removed
1/2 cup parsley, chopped
2 teaspoons lemon zest

SERVES 2 TO 4

Preheat oven to 400°F.

Drain tofu and put it on a plate lined with paper towels and cover with a cloth and heavy can for 20 minutes and then slice tofu into quarter inch slices.

Mix together vinegar, crushed garlic and a pinch of salt and pepper and marinate tofu for 30 minutes.

On a baking sheet roast tofu for 15 minutes. Turn tofu over and add remaining marinade as well as the tomatoes and roast an additional 15 minutes.

To make gremolata, mix together the parsley, lemon zest and minced garlic. Remove tofu and tomatoes from oven and sprinkle with the gremolata mixture!

Great served over quinoa or brown rice!

Roasted Poblano Peppers Stuffed With Smoked Tofu

SERVES 4 TO 6

6 small poblano peppers, cut down the middle lengthwise, seeds removed
1 teaspoon olive oil
1 small yellow onion, peeled and chopped
2 cups smoked tofu, cut into small cubes
1 12- to 14-ounce can black beans, drained & rinsed
1 large tomato, diced
1 cup fresh corn kernels
1/2 tablespoon cumin
1/2 tablespoon chipotle chili powder
1 cup shredded vegan pepper jack or cheddar cheese
1 fresh lime
1/2 cup cilantro or parsley, chopped
salt & pepper to taste

Set oven to broil. Place the peppers skin side down on a foil lined baking sheet and broil 5 minutes, to start the softening. Remove from heat.

Turn oven down to 400°F.

Heat 1 teaspoon of olive oil in a large sauté pan. Add diced onion and cook until soft, about 5 minutes. Add the tofu, black beans, tomato, corn, cumin, chipotle chili powder and a pinch of salt and pepper. Stir to combine and cook until heated through.

Spoon the filling into each pepper half and sprinkle the cheese over each pepper. Bake for 20 minutes. Top with cilantro or parsley and a squeeze of lime.

Burgers

Vegan Quinoa & Lentil Burgers with Sriracha

Black Bean & Three Pepper Burgers

Quick Chickpea & Spinach Burgers

Vegan Quinoa & Lentil Burgers with Sriracha

1 cup red quinoa
1/2 cup dry lentils
1/4 cup quinoa flakes
2 teaspoons curry powder
1 teaspoon cumin
1 teaspoon paprika
1/2 cup parsley, chopped
1/2 cup scallion, chopped
Sriracha (or your favorite chili sauce)
1/2 cup extra virgin olive oil
salt & pepper to taste

In a sauce pan, combine quinoa, lentils, quinoa flakes, curry powder, cumin, paprika and 3 1/2 cups water. Bring to a boil and then lower to a simmer for 15 minutes. Water will be absorbed and the lentils tender.

Put mixture into a bowl and add scallions and fresh herbs. Add Sriracha to your desired spiciness! Salt and pepper to taste. Using your hands, form mixture into patties.

Heat sauté pan and add a little oil for each batch of burgers. Once oil is hot, cook burgers on medium heat for about 4 minutes on each side.

MAKES 8 BURGERS

You will be surprised how little you'll miss meat when you start whipping up delicious vegan burgers. This is a particular favorite of mine, and they freeze well!

Black Bean & Three Pepper Burgers

MAKES 8 BURGERS

1 tablespoon flax seeds
3 tablespoons water
4 tablespoons extra virgin olive oil
1 small sweet onion, chopped small
1/2 red pepper, seeded and chopped small
1/2 yellow pepper, seeded and chopped small
1/2 orange pepper seeded and chopped small
6 cups cooked black beans, drained
2 tablespoons cilantro, chopped
2 tablespoons gluten-free flour
salt & pepper to taste

Make flax "egg" by combing flax seed with 3 tablespoons of water and let sit for 15 minutes.

In a sauté pan, heat two teaspoons olive oil. On medium heat sauté onions and peppers about 5 minutes or until soft. Remove from heat.

In the bowl of a food processor, pulse the beans, pepper and onion mixture, cilantro, flour and flax "egg" until slightly chunky and slightly smooth. Salt and pepper to taste.

Form into patties. Wipe sauté pan and add another 2 teaspoons of oil. Cook patties for about 5 minutes on each side!

SUPERFOOD NOTE:
FLAX SEEDS ARE LOADED WITH PLANT-BASED OMEGA-3S. ALSO USED AS A THICKENING AGENT.

Quick Chickpea & Spinach Burgers

1 tablespoon flax seeds
3 tablespoons water
2 cans garbanzo beans, drained
1 carrot, peeled and grated
1/2 cup parsley, chopped
1 cup fresh spinach, cleaned and chopped
2 teaspoons chili powder (optional)
salt & pepper to taste
extra virgin olive oil for cooking

Make flax "egg" by combing flax seed with 3 tablespoons of water and let sit for 15 minutes.

In a food processor, combine beans, vegetables and spices. Add flax "egg." Pulse so that mixture is part chunky and part smooth. Form into patties. Heat 2 tablespoons of oil in a sauté pan and cook the burgers for 4 to 5 minutes on each side.

MAKES 8 BURGERS

You won't miss the meat at all...

BURGERS

Juices

Blending vs. Juicing

When you blend something, you're consuming those foods in their entirety. So, if you blend up an apple and a cup of spinach, you still have an entire apple and a whole cup of spinach.

When you juice, on the other hand, the fibrous portion of the fruit or vegetable is removed. And, what you're left with are the micronutrients (and the sugars), in a liquid form. For example, juice 4 apples, a bunch of kale and 3 cucumbers and you'll get the micronutrients from those fruits and veggies, but you won't get full the way you would if you blended them into a smoothie, or tried to sit down and eat them all. It would be very difficult to eat an entire pound of kale!

Juicing is a great opportunity to get all the nutrients of a big bunch of greens, and it tastes amazing even with only a tiny bit of fruit to sweeten. But if you only like sweet juices, I'd skip juicing and have a smoothie or piece of fruit!

Is There Kale in my Teeth?
Five Pounds of Veggies
Instant Hydration
Superfuel
Electric Lemonade
Love Your Liver
Liquid Prozac
Bodacious Buzz
Instant Immunity

JUICES

Get your daily dose of antioxidants!

Is There Kale in my Teeth?

MAKES ABOUT 16 OUNCES

Start with a smidge of cayenne and go from there!

2 bunches kale, cleaned
2 big handfuls spinach, cleaned
1 cucumber, rinsed, peel on
3 celery stalks, cleaned and rinsed
1 apple, quartered, rinsed (seeds included)
1 finger ginger, peeled
1/2 lemon, peeled and quartered
1 drop liquid cayenne or 1/8 teaspoon ground cayenne

Juice all ingredients.

Five Pounds of Veggies

1 pound spinach, cleaned
1 pound golden beets, peeled and chopped
3 bunches swiss chard, cleaned (stems included)
1 bunch celery, cleaned (leaves included)
1 pound cucumber, cleaned
1 pound carrot, cleaned and peeled
1 lemon, peeled and cut in quarters

Run all ingredients through your juicer and enjoy!

MAKES ABOUT 16 OUNCES

You can get your daily dose of veggies in one 16-ounce glass of juice!

Instant Hydration

MAKES ABOUT 16 OUNCES

Coconut water is extremely hydrating. It's low in calories, naturally fat- and cholesterol free, and is a great source of potassium!

2 cups fresh pineapple, chopped
1 medium cucumber, peeled and quartered lengthwise
6 ounces coconut water

Juice pineapple and cucumber. Combine mixture with coconut water.

Superfuel

3 cups fresh watermelon, seeds, rind and all
2 cups fresh pineapple, chopped
1/4 lemon, peeled
1 sprig mint

Juice watermelon, pineapple and lemon. When serving, stir in the mint.

MAKES ABOUT 16 OUNCES

JUICES

JUICES

Electric Lemonade

MAKES ABOUT 16 OUNCES

You can actually make this juice without a juicer! Just freshly squeeze the lemons or use 1/3 cup of fresh lemon juice.

2 lemons, peeled and quartered
10 ounces coconut water
1 tablespoon agave, more if needed
1 drop liquid cayenne or 1/8 teaspoon ground cayenne
1 mint sprig

Juice lemons; mix with coconut water, agave and cayenne. When serving, garnish with a mint sprig.

Love Your Liver

1 pound red beets, cleaned and peeled
1 pound carrots, cleaned and peeled
1 apple, cleaned and quartered
1 finger ginger, peeled

Juice all ingredients.

MAKES ABOUT 16 OUNCES

Beets are a huge detoxifier for the liver. This is a go-to drink when you are feeling hungover!

Liquid Prozac

MAKES ABOUT 16 OUNCES

Red peppers are chock-full of magnesium which is a mood elevator and can lessen feelings of anxiety. This is my all-natural, low sodium V8!

1 red pepper, seeded, cleaned and cut into strips
1 tomato, seeded and cut into quarters
1 cucumber, cleaned and quartered
2 celery stalks, cleaned
1/2 lemon, peeled and quartered
1 drop liquid cayenne or 1/8 teaspoon ground cayenne
sea salt

Juice everything and add the sea salt to taste.

Bodacious Buzz

1 pound carrots, peeled and cleaned
2 apples, cleaned and quartered (seeds included)
1 finger ginger, peeled
1 teaspoon liquid Vitamin C or Propolis

Juice all ingredients.

MAKES ABOUT 16 OUNCES

The combination of carrot and ginger will give you an instant buzz that simulates caffeine. Propolis is a liquid Vitamin C found in health food stores. You can always use powder, but it may taste a little grainy.

JUICES

JUICES

Instant Immunity

MAKES ABOUT 16 OUNCES

The combination of orange, grapefruit and lemon juice deliver a triple-threat Vitamin C-packed punch for your immune system!

2 ruby red grapefruit, peeled and cut into sections
2 medium oranges, peeled and cut into sections
1 lemon, peeled and quartered
1 finger ginger, peeled

Juice all ingredients.

Smoothies

Green to be Lean
The Missi!
Power Pina Colada
Dark Chocolate Madness
Bountiful Berry
Wake Up and Smell the Coffee Smoothie

Green to be Lean

MAKES APPROXIMATELY 16 OUNCES

You won't believe how delicious this super green smoothie is. This is my go-to breakfast when I work long days.

1/2 frozen banana
4 coconut water ice cubes
1 handful of spinach
1 handful of raw kale, stems removed
1 handful of swiss chard
1/4 avocado
12 ounces almond milk

Puree all ingredients in blender or Vitamix.

The Missi!

1/2 frozen banana
4 coconut water ice cubes
1 tablespoon almond butter
1 heaping tablespoon of your favorite vegan vanilla protein powder
1 teaspoon flax seed
1 teaspoon hemp seed
12 ounces almond milk

Puree all the ingredients in blender or Vitamix.

MAKES APPROXIMATELY 16 OUNCES

Named after my friend Missi Harnell who teaches Blast900, a "kick your butt" class in Atlanta. Missi says this is the perfect combo of foods after a hard cardio workout!

SUPERFOOD NOTE:
HEMP SEEDS ARE HIGH IN PROTEIN! THEY CONTAIN ALL THE ESSENTIAL AMINO ACIDS NEEDED FOR GROWTH AND REPAIR.

SMOOTHIES

Power Pina Colada

1 cup frozen pineapple
1 cup frozen mango
1/2 frozen banana
2 teaspoons unsweetened dried coconut
1 heaping tablespoon Vega Vanilla protein powder
12 ounces coconut water

Blend all ingredients in blender or Vitamix.

MAKES APPROXIMATELY 16 OUNCES

Dark Chocolate Madness

MAKES APPROXIMATELY 16 OUNCES

Rich and delicious, this healthy chocolate shake tastes so good, even my picky kid will drink it! The avocado gives it a creamy texture.

1 small handful spinach, cleaned
1 leaf kale, cleaned
1 leaf swiss chard, cleaned
1 teaspoon flax seed
1 teaspoon hemp seed
1 heaping teaspoon cacao
1 teaspoon cacao nibs
1 heaping tablespoon Vega (or your favorite) chocolate protein powder
4 coconut water ice cubes
12 ounces chocolate almond milk

Blend all ingredients in blender or Vitamix.

SUPERFOOD NOTE:
CACAO LOWERS BLOOD PRESSURE AND IMPROVES BLOOD FLOW TO YOUR BRAIN AND HEART!

SMOOTHIES

Bountiful Berry

MAKES APPROXIMATELY 16 OUNCES

I love this smoothie in the heat of summer because the berries are at their peak and I feel super hydrated adding the coconut water. Plus, berries are filled with high levels of antioxidants and the camu berry is one of the most abundant sources of Vitamin C available. One serving has 60 times more Vitamin C than an orange!

1/2 cup frozen blackberries
1/2 cup frozen blueberries
1/2 cup frozen raspberries
1/2 frozen banana
1/4 teaspoon camu powder
12 ounces coconut water

Puree all ingredients in blender or Vitamix.

Wake Up and Smell the Coffee Smoothie

MAKES APPROXIMATELY 16 OUNCES

5 coconut water ice cubes
1 cup almond milk
1 cup cold brew coffee or chilled coffee
1 tablespoon almond butter
1/2 teaspoon flax seed
1/2 teaspoon hemp seed
1/2 teaspoon maca (optional)
1 scoop protein powder (optional)

Put ingredients in blender or Vitamix in the order listed. Blend on high until smooth.

SUPERFOOD NOTE:
MACA IS A ROOT VEGETABLE GROWN IN THE ANDES AND GROUND INTO POWDER. IT'S USED TO BOOST ENERGY AND ENDURANCE.

Gluten-Free Baking

Raw Brownies

A Great Muffin Base

Gluten-free Chocolate Chip Cookies

The Best Gluten-free Vegan Peanut Butter Chocolate Chunk Cookies Ever

Chocolate Cherry Oatmeal Cookies

Raw Power Bar

Chewy Coconut Date Bars

Chocolate Chunk Banana Bread

Vegan Crispy Rice Treats

Easy Coconut Macaroons

Yummy Pumpkin Bread

GLUTEN-FREE BAKING

Raw Brownies

MAKES APPROXIMATELY 12 BROWNIES

I like to use small individual molds to make pretty shapes for my brownies! These are very rich!

2 cups raw almonds
1 cup raw pecans or walnuts
2 cups dates, pitted
2/3 cup cacao powder
2 teaspoons, plus extra water
2 teaspoons pure vanilla extract
pinch of salt

Pulse all ingredients in food processor until you have a sticky, dough-like mixture. If it seems too dry and is not coming together, add water.

Line a 6 x 6-inch cake pan with parchment paper and press brownies evenly into pan. Refrigerate at least 3 hours and cut in small squares.

A Great Muffin Base

4 cups gluten-free flour (Pamela's is my favorite!)
4 teaspoons baking soda
4 teaspoons baking powder
1 teaspoon salt
1 teaspoon cinnamon
1 teaspoon ginger powder
1 2/3 cup almond milk
1 2/3 cup maple syrup
1 cup extra virgin olive oil

MAKES 12 MUFFINS

Preheat oven to 325°F.

Combine dry ingredients together in one bowl and wet in another. Slowly pour wet ingredients into the dry until combined. Don't over mix.

Add in your mix-ins.*

Pre-grease your muffin tins and fill a little over half way. Bake for 15 minutes. Rotate muffin pan and bake for an additional 5 minutes.

*Here is my list of favorite mix-in combinations for your muffins!

- 1/2 cup vegan chocolate chips and 1/2 cup fresh raspberries
- 1/2 cup vegan chocolate chips and 1 small banana, chopped fine
- 1 apple, cored and chopped fine and 1/2 cup toasted walnuts
- 1 cup blueberries and 2 tablespoons lemon zest
- 1/2 cup dates, chopped fine and 1/2 cup chopped walnuts or pecans
- 1/2 cup vegan chocolate chips, 1/4 cup toasted, flaked coconut and 1/2 cup goji berries

SUPERFOOD NOTE:
GOJI BERRIES ARE USED BY CHINESE HERBALISTS TO INCREASE CIRCULATION AND BOOST THE IMMUNE SYSTEM!

Gluten-Free Chocolate Chip Cookies

MAKES 12 MEDIUM COOKIES

7 tablespoons Earth Balance "butter"
1 tablespoon extra virgin olive oil
1/2 cup organic sugar
1 flax "egg" (1 tablespoon ground flax seed mixed with three tablespoons water)
1 teaspoon pure vanilla extract
1/2 teaspoon gluten-free baking soda
1/2 teaspoon salt
1 cup gluten-free quick oats
1 cup almond flour
1/4 teaspoon cinnamon
3/4 cup vegan chocolate chips

Preheat oven to 350°F.

In a mixer, cream Earth Balance and extra virgin olive oil. Add the sugar and flax "egg". Slowly add dry ingredients to incorporate and then fold in chips.

Using a small scoop, drop onto a greased cookie sheet. Bake for 15 minutes or until golden brown.

The Best Gluten-Free Vegan Peanut Butter Chocolate Chunk Cookies Ever

MAKES 12 COOKIES

1/4 cup Earth Balance "butter"
1/4 cup organic, smooth peanut butter
1/4 cup brown sugar
1/3 cup organic cane sugar
1 flax "egg" (1 tablespoon ground flax seed mixed with 3 tablespoons water)
1 teaspoon vanilla
1/2 teaspoon gluten-free baking powder
1/2 teaspoon gluten-free baking soda
1 cup gluten-free oat flour
1 cup almond flour
1 cup vegan chocolate chunks

Pre-heat oven to 350°F. In mixer, cream together Earth Balance and peanut butter. Slowly add sugars, the flax "egg" and the vanilla. Slowly add dry ingredients. Fold in chunks.

Using an ice cream scoop, drop onto a greased cookie sheet. Bake for 15 minutes.

GLUTEN-FREE BAKING

GLUTEN-FREE BAKING

Chocolate Cherry Oatmeal Cookies

MAKES ABOUT 2 DOZEN

2/3 cup applesauce
1/2 cup vegetable oil
2 teaspoons vanilla extract
1 1/2 cup organic cane sugar
2 tablespoons ground flax seed
1 1/2 cup gluten-free flour (Pamela's is my favorite!)
2/3 cup vegan baking powder
1 teaspoon salt
2 cups gluten-free rolled oats
1 cup vegan chocolate chips
1 cup sun dried cherries or cranberries

Preheat oven to 350°F. In a mixer, combine wet ingredients together. In a separate bowl, mix all dry ingredients. Slowly fold in the dry ingredients to the wet. Using a small scoop, drop dough onto a greased or parchment covered cookie sheet. With the palm of your hand, press each cookie down a little bit. These cookies don't spread out very much, so you can place them pretty close together. Bake for 15 minutes.

Raw Power Bar

MAKES APPROXIMATELY 24 BARS

1 cup raw walnuts
1 cup raw almonds
1 1/2 cup raw pumpkin seeds
2/3 cup chia seeds
2/3 cup flax seeds
2/3 cup hemp seeds
1/2 cup cacao nibs
1 cup golden raisins
2 cups Medjool dates, pitted
1/2 cup organic coconut, flaked
4 tablespoons coconut oil
3/4 cup candied ginger
1/2 teaspoon ground ginger

Reserve a small amount of each ingredient to fold in at the end.

Puree all ingredients in the food processor until sticky and pulls together. Fold in the reserved ingredients, so you can see seeds and fruits.

Press into a parchment covered baking pan or molds and freeze to set for 2 hours. Cut into bars or pieces.

SUPERFOOD NOTE:
CHIA SEEDS are packed with omega-3 fatty acids, fiber and calcium. Also used as a thickening agent.

Chewy Coconut Date Bars

MAKES APPROXIMATELY 24 BARS

1 cup smooth organic peanut butter
2/3 cup pure maple syrup
2/3 cup brown rice syrup
2 tablespoons coconut oil, melted
2 teaspoons pure vanilla or coconut extract
1 teaspoon salt
4 cups rolled oats
2 cups vegan rice crisps
1 1/2 cups unsweetened shredded coconut
1 cup dates, pitted and coarsely chopped

Pre-heat oven to 350°F. In 2 bowls, mix the wet and the dry ingredients separately. Slowly add the dry ingredients to the wet and mix until combined. On a parchment covered baking pan, spread mixture evenly. Bake for about 20 minutes. Cut into bars.

Chocolate Chunk Banana Bread

3 super ripe bananas
1 teaspoon vanilla extract
1/4 cup almond butter
2 flax "eggs" (2 tablespoon ground flax seed mixed with 6 tablespoons water)
1/2 cup coconut flour
1/2 teaspoon baking soda
1/2 teaspoon baking powder
1/2 teaspoon cinnamon
1/4 teaspoon salt
1 cup dark chocolate chunks

SERVES 12

Preheat oven to 350°F. Line a 8 x 4-inch or 9 x 5-inch loaf pan with parchment paper and spray with nonstick cooking spray.

In the bowl of an electric mixer, combine bananas, vanilla and almond butter; mix until well combined, smooth and creamy. Add in flax "eggs" and mix on medium speed until combined. With the mixer on medium-low speed, add in coconut flour, baking soda, baking powder, cinnamon and salt; mix again until just combined. Gently fold in chocolate chips.

Pour batter into prepared pan and smooth top. Bake for 30 to 40 minutes or until tester inserted into center comes out clean. Remove from oven and place on wire rack to cool for 20 minutes, then carefully invert, remove bread from pan and place back on wire rack to cool completely. Cut into 12 slices.

GLUTEN-FREE BAKING

Vegan Crispy Rice Treats

MAKES APPROXIMATELY 12 SQUARES

1/2 cup maple syrup
1/2 cup brown rice syrup
1/2 cup almond butter
2 tablespoons coconut oil
1/4 teaspoon salt
4 cups gluten-free rice crisps (plain or chocolate)
1 cup vegan chocolate chips

In a saucepan, bring maple and rice syrup to a boil for 1 minute, stirring frequently. Remove from heat and stir in almond butter, coconut oil and salt until smooth. Fold in rice cereal and chocolate chips.

On a parchment lined 6 x 9-inch pan press mixture evenly. Set in refrigerator for at least an hour. Cut into squares.

Easy Coconut Macaroons

3 cups unsweetened shredded coconut
1 1/2 cups sweetened condensed coconut milk
1/2 teaspoon vanilla extract

Preheat oven to 300°F, and line a baking sheet with parchment paper or a Silpat. Combine all of the ingredients in a medium bowl, and mix until well combined. This is a good time to taste-test your batter, and adjust the sweetness to your taste. Drop mixture by the tablespoon approximately an inch and a half apart. Bake for 12 to 15 minutes.

MAKES 32 PIECES

Yummy Pumpkin Bread

SERVES 12

1/4 cup non-dairy milk
1/4 teaspoon lemon juice
15 ounces canned pumpkin
1 cup brown sugar
2 tablespoons pure maple syrup
2 teaspoons vanilla extract
2 cups whole wheat flour
1 teaspoon baking soda
1 teaspoon pumpkin pie spice
1/2 teaspoon baking powder

Preheat oven to 350°F. Grease a standard loaf pan pan with olive oil or coconut oil. Whisk non-dairy milk and lemon juice together until bubbly and set aside. In a medium mixing bowl, cream pumpkin, sugar, syrup and extract together. In a large bowl, whisk flour, baking soda, pumpkin pie spice and baking powder together.

Add both wet mixtures into dry mixture and stir until just combined. Pour into loaf pan, using a spatula to evenly distribute and smooth out the top. Grab a large piece of aluminum foil and make a tent over the pan. Bake for 1 hour, or until a toothpick inserted in the center comes out clean. Once the bread has cooled but is still slightly warm, gently remove it from the pan and on to a serving plate.

Fun Stuff

Super Seed Crackers

Coconut Bacon

Three Quick Dressings

The Best Hummus I've Ever Had!!!

Crazy Good Granola

Super Seed Crackers

1/2 cup brown rice flour
1 cup raw hulled sunflower seeds
1/4 cup hemp seeds
1/4 cup raw pepitas (pumpkin seeds)
1/4 cup white sesame seeds
2 tablespoons black sesame seeds or more white sesame seeds
2 tablespoons whole chia seeds
3 tablespoons ground chia seeds
1 1/4 teaspoons garlic powder
1 large clove garlic, grated on a microplane
1 cup yellow onion, peeled and grated on a microplane
2 teaspoons dried oregano
1 teaspoon coconut sugar or natural cane sugar
1 teaspoon dried basil
3/4 teaspoon fine sea salt, or to taste
1/8 teaspoon cayenne pepper, or to taste (optional)
1 1/2 cup cup hot water

MAKES 24 CRACKERS

I'm a carb addict, but these gluten-free and vegan crunchy delights satisfy my cracker cravings. To make ground chia seed, in a coffee grinder or high-speed blender, grind 1/2 cup chia seeds on high until a fine powder forms. Store any unused ground chia seed in the fridge in an airtight container.

Heat the oven to 300°F. Line two standard baking sheets or one extra-large baking sheet with parchment paper.

In a large bowl, stir together all of the dry ingredients. Add the hot water and mix well.

Transfer half the seed mixture to each baking sheet (or if using one extra-large baking sheet, spoon all of it onto the sheet). With your hands, spread the mixture starting in the center and pushing outward, until you form a large, misshapen rectangle, no more than 1/4 inch thick. The mixture will be very wet, but this is normal. Be sure that the dough is uniform in thickness and the corners aren't too thick. Bake for 30 minutes.

Remove the baking sheet(s) from the over and using a pizza cutter, carefully slice the dough into large crackers. Carefully flip each cracker using a spatula or your hands. Don't worry if a couple break here and there! If for some reason the crackers are sticking to the parchment paper, just leave them as is and remove them after the second bake.

Return the baking sheet(s) to the oven and bake for 23 to 25 minutes more, until the crackers are golden. Watch closely during the last 5 to 10 minutes of baking to ensure they don't burn. Remove from the oven and let cool on the baking sheet(s) for 5 minutes. Transfer the crackers to a couple of cooling racks and let cool completely.

Store the cooled crackers in a paper bag on the counter or in an airtight container in the fridge for up to 1 week. You can also store them in a freezer-safe zip-top bag in the freezer for 3 to 4 weeks. If the crackers soften while storing (this can happen in humid environments), toast in the oven at 300°F for 5 to 7 minutes, then let cool completely. This is usually enough to return their former crispness!

FUN STUFF

FUN STUFF

Coconut Bacon

MAKES 2 CUPS

Oh my god, this stuff is delicious on EVERYTHING! I love it tossed in salads, sprinkled over soups and just as a snack. Also terrific over roasted vegetables. It really gives you that bacon texture and taste, but is a true superfood! Try it, you'll be addicted.

2 cups flaked, unsweetened coconut
1 tablespoon liquid smoke
1 tablespoon gluten-free tamari
1 tablespoon maple syrup
sea salt
freshly ground pepper

Preheat oven to 325°F. Toss first 4 ingredients together and spread out on a baking sheet that is greased or lined with parchment paper. Bake for 20 minutes.

Remove from the oven and season with sea salt and pepper. The mixture will be hard. Remove from baking sheet and let cool on a plate. When cool to the touch, break up into pieces and store in an airtight container. It will be good for a week, but there's no way it will last that long!

Three Quick Dressings

Jenny's Every Day Dressing

MAKES ALMOST A CUP

1 teaspoon Dijon mustard
1 clove garlic, peeled and pressed
4 teaspoons balsamic vinegar
2 tablespoons white balsamic vinegar
2 teaspoons Worchestershire sauce
3/4 cup extra virgin olive oil
salt & pepper to taste

In a glass jar with a lid, place the mustard and garlic. Add oil, vinegars, Worchestershire sauce and a little salt and pepper. Shake vigorously.

I love this quick and easy dressing because I always have these ingredients on hand and can whip it up in less than 5 minutes. This is great on any green salad!

Fresh Lemon Dressing

MAKES JUST OVER 3/4 CUP

1 bunch flat leaf parsley, stems removed
2 cloves garlic, peeled
juice of one fresh lemon
3/4 cup extra virgin olive oil
salt & pepper to taste

In a food processor or Vitamix, combine parsley, garlic and lemon With the machine still running, slowly add olive oil. Add salt and pepper to taste.

This dressing is great tossed with fresh asparagus or over any gluten-free grain and vegetables!

Miso Dressing

MAKES 1/4 CUP

1 1/2 tablespoon red miso paste
3 tablespoons rice wine vinegar
1 tablespoon honey
1 tablespoon fresh ginger, peeled and grated
2 teaspoons fresh lime juice

In a bowl, whisk miso into vinegar and then slowly whisk in the rest of the ingredients! That's it!

I love to drizzle this over hot roasted vegetables. Yum!

HAPPY, BE!
ARE A TABLE WITH A STRANGER!
ENJOY YOUR MEAL THE WAY IT WAS MADE, SLOW & WITH CARE

ESPRESSO
CAPPUCCINO..... $3
LATTE $3
HOT TEA $2.50

DESSERT OF THE DAY $3
HOMEMADE CAKES $6

FUN STUFF

The Best Hummus I've Ever Had!!!

1 cup dried chickpeas
2 teaspoons baking soda, divided
4 garlic cloves, unpeeled
1/3 cup (or more) fresh lemon juice
1 teaspoon kosher salt, plus more
2/3 cup good quality tahini (I love Soom Tehina, available on Amazon)
1/4 teaspoon ground cumin
olive oil, for serving
chopped parsley and paprika, for serving (optional)

Place the chickpeas in a large bowl with 1 teaspoon of the baking soda and cover with plenty of water. (The chickpeas will double in volume, so use more water than you think you need.) Soak the chickpeas overnight at room temperature. The next day, drain the chickpeas and rinse under cold water.

Place the chickpeas in a large pot with the remaining 1 teaspoon baking soda and add cold water to cover by at least 4 inches. Bring the chickpeas to a boil over high heat, skimming off any scum that rises to the surface. Lower the heat to medium, cover the pot, and continue to simmer for about 1 hour, until the chickpeas are completely tender. Then simmer them a little more. (The secret to creamy hummus is overcooked chickpeas; so don't worry if they are mushy and falling apart a little.) Drain.

Meanwhile, process garlic, lemon juice, and 1 teaspoon salt in a food processor until coarsely puréed; let sit 10 minutes to allow garlic to mellow.

Strain garlic mixture through a fine-mesh sieve into a small bowl, pressing on solids to release as much liquid as possible. Return liquid to food processor; discard solids. Add tahini and pulse to combine. With motor running, add 1/4 cup ice water by the tablespoonful and process (it may seize up at first) until mixture is very smooth, pale, and thick. Add chickpeas and cumin and purée for several minutes, until the hummus is smooth and creamy. Then purée it some more! Taste and adjust the seasoning with salt, lemon juice, and cumin, if you like.

To serve, spread the hummus in a shallow bowl, dust with paprika, top with parsley and more tehina sauce, and drizzle generously with oil.

MAKES ABOUT 3 CUPS

This recipe is 100% stolen from one of my favorite Israeli chef's, Michael Solomonov. I can't believe the difference between this whipped and creamy hummus and the hummus I have been eating for years. You'll never eat store bought hummus again!

Crazy Good Granola

MAKES ABOUT 7 CUPS

This granola is gluten-free, paleo, vegan and is yummy over almond milk yogurt or as a snack after a heavy workout.

1 cup raw sunflower seeds, shelled
1 cup raw pumpkin seeds
1 cup sliced, raw almonds
1 cup raw pecan pieces
1 cup raw cashews, chopped
1 cup shredded coconut
15 dates, pitted and chopped
1/4 cup coconut oil, melted
2 teaspoons cinnamon
3 teaspoons vanilla
kosher salt

Heat oven to 325°F. Toss all seeds, nuts, shredded coconut and dates in a medium bowl. Mix melted coconut oil with cinnamon, vanilla and a pinch of salt. Add oil mixture to seeds and mix until well coated. Spread onto a baking sheet lined with parchment paper. Bake for 20 minutes and then stir the granola to make sure it's cooking evenly. Bake another 5 minutes. Remove and cool. Break up granola and store in an airtight container.

SPECIAL THANKS

Ten years later, it still takes a village!

There is no question that this third labor of love would never have happened without the dream team that started this adventure with me just over 10 years ago. I am so fortunate to have the original three, plus a new super hero who worked together to create this book with me.

BreeAnne Clowdus, you are a magnificent, inspired human being. You were able to capture my spirit perfectly in our very memorable photo shoot. Who knew that drinking vodka at 10 AM could inspire such comfort and creativity! (For me, I mean!) Thank you for jumping into our project and creating the lovely cover photo for this book.

She hates being overly recognized, but Hope Mirlis, none of this would ever have come to fruition without your continual support, incredible diligence and gentle nudging! Thank you for taking on the editing portion of this latest endeavor and keeping all of us on track. You have a wonderful way of making me believe I am capable even on days when I don't believe it myself. I can't wait for our next adventure!

Joel Silverman is a foodie friend and has been the photographer on the cookbooks from the start. Your attention to detail always amazes me and you elevated my food to a level that makes me crave vegan food daily! Thank you for your patience with my more limited knowledge of the time and skill it takes to capture exquisite food photos. I am honored to now have a picture of your mother and your father in our work together.

Angela Aquino, I love your aesthetic every time you put your designs in front of me! Whether it's designing fun websites for our Planet Jenny businesses or creating our cookbooks, your colors, layouts and artwork fit perfectly. Thank you for understanding and believing in my overall vision and laying it out in a beautiful, thoughtful way.

In addition to the dream team, there are forty-something employees and my entire family and tribe that make it possible for me to take the time away from our daily operation to explore all of my passions and interests. Thank you, thank you, thank you from the bottom of my heart.

Jenny

INDEX

A
almond milk
- Dark Chocolate Madness 91
- Great Muffin Base, A 100
- Green to Be Lean 87
- Missi, The! 88
- Wake Up and Smell the Coffee Smoothie 94

almonds
- Crazy Good Granola 123
- Raw Brownies 99
- Raw Kale & Swiss Chard Slaw with Golden Raisins, Dates, Toasted Almonds & Fresh Herb Dressing 29
- Raw Power Bar 106

apples
- Bodacious Buzz 80
- Is There Kale in my Teeth? 71
- Love Your Liver 78
- Raw Collard, Apple, Sun Dried Figs & Candied Ginger with Apple Cider Vinaigrette 32
- Roasted Golden Beets, Cauliflower and Apples with Honey Dijon Dressing 33

avocados
- Juicy Jenny Collard Wraps 52
- My Favorite Vegetable Tacos with Tomatillos & Pico De Gallo 53
- Red Quinoa, Fresh Corn, Blistered Tomatoes & Avocado 40

B
bananas
- Chocolate Chunk Banana Bread 108

beans
- Black Bean & Three Pepper Burgers 65
- Golden Quinoa with Grilled Stone Fruit, Butter Beans, Spring Onions & Fresh Lemon Dressing 39
- Jenny's Gypsy Soup 24
- Quinoa & Fava Bean Chili 17
- Roasted Red Poblano Peppers Stuffed with Smoked Tofu 61

beets
- Five Pounds of Veggies 72
- Love Your Liver 78
- Raw Six Vegetable Spiralized Salad with Green Tahini Dressing 35
- Roasted Golden Beets, Cauliflower and Apples with Honey Dijon Dressing 33

berries
- Bountiful Berry 93

Best Gluten-Free Vegan Peanut Butter Chocolate Chunk Cookies Ever, The 102
Best Hummus I've Ever Had, The!!! 122
Black Bean & Three Pepper Burgers 65
Bodacious Buzz 80
Bountiful Berry 93
Braised Turnips with Miso 47
Brussels sprouts
- Roasted Rainbow 45

burgers
- Black Bean & Three Pepper Burgers 65
- Quick Chickpea & Spinach Burgers 66
- Vegan Quinoa & Lentil Burgers with Sriracha 64

C
cacao
- Dark Chocolate Madness 91
- Raw Brownies 99

carrots
- Bodacious Buzz 80
- Creamy Cauliflower Soup 23
- Five Pounds of Veggies 72
- Jenny's Gypsy Soup 24
- Love Your Liver 78
- Raw Six Vegetable Spiralized Salad with Green Tahini Dressing 35
- Roasted Rainbow 45

cashews
- Kale Caesar with Cherry Tomato, Cucumber & Mock Parmesan 30

cauliflower
- Creamy Cauliflower Soup 23
- Roasted Golden Beets, Cauliflower and Apples with Honey Dijon Dressing 33

celery
- Creamy Cauliflower Soup 23
- Five Pounds of Veggies 72
- Is There Kale in my Teeth? 71
- Liquid Prozac 79

chard, swiss
- Dark Chocolate Madness 91
- Five Pounds of Veggies 72
- Green to Be Lean 87
- Jeweled Quinoa with Sautéed Greens, Portobello Mushrooms & Sautéed Tamari Tofu 36
- Raw Kale & Swiss Chard Slaw with Golden Raisins, Dates, Toasted Almonds & Fresh Herb Dressing 29

cheese, vegan
- Roasted Red Poblano Peppers Stuffed with Smoked Tofu 61
- Vegan "Chicken" Tortilla Soup 21

cherries
- Chocolate Cherry Oatmeal Cookies 105

Chewy Coconut Date Bars 107
chickpeas
- Best Hummus I've Ever Had, The!!! 122
- Jenny's Gypsy Soup 24
- Quick Chickpea & Spinach Burgers 66

Chocolate Cherry Oatmeal Cookies 105
chocolate chips/chunks
- Best Gluten-Free Vegan Peanut Butter Chocolate Chunk Cookies Ever, The 102
- Chocolate Cherry Oatmeal Cookies 105
- Chocolate Chunk Banana Bread 108
- Gluten-Free Chocolate Chip Cookies 101
- Vegan Crispy Rice Treats 111

Chocolate Chunk Banana Bread 108
coconut
- Chewy Coconut Date Bars 107
- Coconut Bacon 119
- Crazy Good Granola 123
- Easy Coconut Macaroons 112

Coconut Bacon 119
coconut milk
- Easy Coconut Macaroons 112

coconut water
- Bountiful Berry 93
- Electric Lemonade 77
- Instant Hydration 73
- Power Pina Colada 90

coffee
- Wake Up and Smell the Coffee Smoothie 94

collards
- Juicy Jenny Collard Wraps 52
- Raw Collard, Apple, Sun Dried Figs & Candied Ginger with Apple Cider Vinaigrette 32

corn
- Red Quinoa, Fresh Corn, Blistered Tomatoes & Avocado 40
- Roasted Red Poblano Peppers Stuffed with Smoked Tofu 61
- Vegan "Chicken" Tortilla Soup 21

Crazy Good Granola 123
Creamy Cauliflower Soup 23
cucumbers
- Five Pounds of Veggies 72
- Instant Hydration 73
- Is There Kale in my Teeth? 71
- Kale Caesar with Cherry Tomato, Cucumber & Mock Parmesan 30
- Liquid Prozac 79

curry
- Grilled Sengalese Tofu with Peanuts, Ginger & Curry 59

INDEX

D
Dark Chocolate Madness 91
dates
　Chewy Coconut Date Bars 107
　Crazy Good Granola 123
　Raw Brownies 99
　Raw Kale & Swiss Chard Slaw with Golden Raisins, Dates, Toasted Almonds & Fresh Herb Dressing 29
　Raw Power Bar 106

E
Easy Coconut Macaroons 112
Electric Lemonade 77

F
figs
　Raw Collard, Apple, Sun Dried Figs & Candied Ginger with Apple Cider Vinaigrette 32
Five Pounds of Veggies 72
Fresh Lemon Dressing 120
fun stuff
　Best Hummus I've Ever Had, The!!! 122
　Coconut Bacon 119
　Crazy Good Granola 123
　Fresh Lemon Dressing 120
　Jenny's Every Day Dressing 120
　Miso Dressing 120
　Super Seed Crackers 116

G
ginger
　Grilled Sengalese Tofu with Peanuts, Ginger & Curry 59
　Raw Collard, Apple, Sun Dried Figs & Candied Ginger with Apple Cider Vinaigrette 32
　Raw Power Bar 106
gluten-free baking
　Best Gluten-Free Vegan Peanut Butter Chocolate Chunk Cookies Ever, The 102
　Chewy Coconut Date Bars 107
　Chocolate Cherry Oatmeal Cookies 105
　Chocolate Chunk Banana Bread 108
　Easy Coconut Macaroons 112
　Gluten-Free Chocolate Chip Cookies 101
　Great Muffin Base, A 100
　Raw Brownies 99
　Raw Power Bar 106
　Vegan Crispy Rice Treats 111
　Yummy Pumpkin Bread 113
Gluten-Free Chocolate Chip Cookies 101

Golden Quinoa with Grilled Stone Fruit, Butter Beans, Spring Onions & Fresh Lemon Dressing 39
grapefruit
　Instant Immunity 83
Great Muffin Base, A 100
Green to Be Lean 87
Grilled Sengalese Tofu with Peanuts, Ginger & Curry 59

H
honey
　Roasted Golden Beets, Cauliflower and Apples with Honey Dijon Dressing 33

I
Instant Hydration 73
Instant Immunity 83
Is There Kale in my Teeth? 71

J
Jenny's Every Day Dressing 120
Jenny's Gypsy Soup 24
Jeweled Quinoa with Sautéed Greens, Portobello Mushrooms & Sautéed Tamari Tofu 36
juices
　Bodacious Buzz 80
　Electric Lemonade 77
　Five Pounds of Veggies 72
　Instant Hydration 73
　Instant Immunity 83
　Is There Kale in my Teeth? 71
　Liquid Prozac 79
　Love Your Liver 78
　Superfuel 74
Juicy Jenny Collard Wraps 52

K
kale
　Dark Chocolate Madness 91
　Green to Be Lean 87
　Is There Kale in my Teeth? 71
　Jeweled Quinoa with Sautéed Greens, Portobello Mushrooms & Sautéed Tamari Tofu 36
　Kale Caesar with Cherry Tomato, Cucumber & Mock Parmesan 30
　Raw Kale & Swiss Chard Slaw with Golden Raisins, Dates, Toasted Almonds & Fresh Herb Dressing 29

Kale Caesar with Cherry Tomato, Cucumber & Mock Parmesan 30

L
lemons/lemon juice
　Electric Lemonade 77
　Fresh Lemon Dressing 120
　Golden Quinoa with Grilled Stone Fruit, Butter Beans, Spring Onions & Fresh Lemon Dressing 39
　Instant Immunity 83
lentils
　Vegan Quinoa & Lentil Burgers with Sriracha 64
Liquid Prozac 79
Love Your Liver 78

M
mangoes
　Power Pina Colada 90
maple syrup
　Great Muffin Base, A 100
millet
　Red & Yellow Peppers Stuffed with Millet Salad 51
miso
　Braised Turnips with Miso 47
　Miso Dressing 120
Miso Dressing 120
Missi, The! 88
mushrooms
　Jenny's Gypsy Soup 24
　Jeweled Quinoa with Sautéed Greens, Portobello Mushrooms & Sautéed Tamari Tofu 36
　My Favorite Vegetable Tacos with Tomatillos & Pico De Gallo 53
　Thai Noodle Bowl 20
　Wild Mushroom Potage 18
mustard, Dijon
　Roasted Golden Beets, Cauliflower and Apples with Honey Dijon Dressing 33
My Favorite Vegetable Tacos with Tomatillos & Pico De Gallo 53

N
noodles
　Thai Noodle Bowl 20

O
oats
　Chocolate Cherry Oatmeal Cookies 105

INDEX

onions
Golden Quinoa with Grilled Stone Fruit, Butter Beans, Spring Onions & Fresh Lemon Dressing 39

oranges
Instant Immunity 83

P

peaches
Golden Quinoa with Grilled Stone Fruit, Butter Beans, Spring Onions & Fresh Lemon Dressing 39

peanuts/peanut butter
Best Gluten-Free Vegan Peanut Butter Chocolate Chunk Cookies Ever, The 102
Grilled Sengalese Tofu with Peanuts, Ginger & Curry 59

pecans
Crazy Good Granola 123
Raw Brownies 99

peppers
Black Bean & Three Pepper Burgers 65
Creamy Cauliflower Soup 23
Liquid Prozac 79
My Favorite Vegetable Tacos with Tomatillos & Pico De Gallo 53
Quinoa & Fava Bean Chili 17
Red & Yellow Peppers Stuffed with Millet Salad 51
Roasted Rainbow 45
Roasted Red Poblano Peppers Stuffed with Smoked Tofu 61
Vegan "Chicken" Tortilla Soup 21

pineapples
Instant Hydration 73
Power Pina Colada 90
Superfuel 74

plums
Golden Quinoa with Grilled Stone Fruit, Butter Beans, Spring Onions & Fresh Lemon Dressing 39
Power Pina Colada 90

pumpkin
Yummy Pumpkin Bread 113

Q

Quick Chickpea & Spinach Burgers 66

quinoa
Golden Quinoa with Grilled Stone Fruit, Butter Beans, Spring Onions & Fresh Lemon Dressing 39
Jeweled Quinoa with Sautéed Greens, Portobello Mushrooms & Sautéed Tamari Tofu 36
Quinoa & Fava Bean Chili 17
Red Quinoa, Fresh Corn, Blistered Tomatoes & Avocado 40
Vegan Quinoa & Lentil Burgers with Sriracha 64

Quinoa & Fava Bean Chili 17

R

radishes, watermelon
Raw Six Vegetable Spiralized Salad with Green Tahini Dressing 35

raisins
Raw Kale & Swiss Chard Slaw with Golden Raisins, Dates, Toasted Almonds & Fresh Herb Dressing 29
Raw Power Bar 106
Red & Yellow Peppers Stuffed with Millet Salad 51

Raw Brownies 99
Raw Collard, Apple, Sun Dried Figs & Candied Ginger with Apple Cider Vinaigrette 32
Raw Kale & Swiss Chard Slaw with Golden Raisins, Dates, Toasted Almonds & Fresh Herb Dressing 29
Raw Power Bar 106
Raw Six Vegetable Spiralized Salad with Green Tahini Dressing 35
Red & Yellow Peppers Stuffed with Millet Salad 51
Red Quinoa, Fresh Corn, Blistered Tomatoes & Avocado 40

rice crisps
Vegan Crispy Rice Treats 111
Roasted Balsamic Tofu with Gremolata & Cherry Tomatoes 60
Roasted Golden Beets, Cauliflower and Apples with Honey Dijon Dressing 33
Roasted Rainbow 45
Roasted Red Poblano Peppers Stuffed with Smoked Tofu 61
Roasted Sweet & Spicy Sweet Potatoes with Romesco Sauce 46

S

salads
Golden Quinoa with Grilled Stone Fruit, Butter Beans, Spring Onions & Fresh Lemon Dressing 39
Jeweled Quinoa with Sautéed Greens, Portobello Mushrooms & Sautéed Tamari Tofu 36
Kale Caesar with Cherry Tomato, Cucumber & Mock Parmesan 30
Raw Collard, Apple, Sun Dried Figs & Candied Ginger with Apple Cider Vinaigrette 32
Raw Kale & Swiss Chard Slaw with Golden Raisins, Dates, Toasted Almonds & Fresh Herb Dressing 29
Raw Six Vegetable Spiralized Salad with Green Tahini Dressing 35
Red Quinoa, Fresh Corn, Blistered Tomatoes & Avocado 40
Roasted Golden Beets, Cauliflower and Apples with Honey Dijon Dressing 33

seeds
Crazy Good Granola 123
Raw Power Bar 106
Super Seed Crackers 116

smoothies
Bountiful Berry 93
Dark Chocolate Madness 91
Green to Be Lean 87
Missi, The! 88
Power Pina Colada 90
Wake Up and Smell the Coffee Smoothie 94

soups
Creamy Cauliflower Soup 23
Jenny's Gypsy Soup 24
Quinoa & Fava Bean Chili 17
Thai Noodle Bowl 20
Vegan "Chicken" Tortilla Soup 21
Wild Mushroom Potage 18

Spaghetti Squash with Summer or Winter Marinara 54

spinach
Dark Chocolate Madness 91
Five Pounds of Veggies 72
Green to Be Lean 87
Is There Kale in my Teeth? 71
Jenny's Gypsy Soup 24
Jeweled Quinoa with Sautéed Greens, Portobello Mushrooms & Sautéed Tamari Tofu 36
Quick Chickpea & Spinach Burgers 66
Red & Yellow Peppers Stuffed with Millet Salad 51
Thai Noodle Bowl 20
Wild Mushroom Potage 18

squash
Jenny's Gypsy Soup 24

Quinoa & Fava Bean Chili 17
Raw Six Vegetable Spiralized Salad with Green Tahini Dressing 35
Roasted Rainbow 45
Spaghetti Squash with Summer or Winter Marinara 54

Sriracha
Vegan Quinoa & Lentil Burgers with Sriracha 64

Summer Marinara 54
Super Seed Crackers 116
Superfuel 74

sweet potatoes
Roasted Sweet & Spicy Sweet Potatoes with Romesco Sauce 46

T

tahini
Best Hummus I've Ever Had, The!!! 122
Raw Six Vegetable Spiralized Salad with Green Tahini Dressing 35

tamari
Jeweled Quinoa with Sautéed Greens, Portobello Mushrooms & Sautéed Tamari Tofu 36

tempeh
Vegan "Chicken" Tortilla Soup 21

Thai Noodle Bowl 20

tofu
Grilled Sengalese Tofu with Peanuts, Ginger & Curry 59
Jeweled Quinoa with Sautéed Greens, Portobello Mushrooms & Sautéed Tamari Tofu 36
Roasted Balsamic Tofu with Gremolata & Cherry Tomatoes 60
Roasted Red Poblano Peppers Stuffed with Smoked Tofu 61
Thai Noodle Bowl 20

tomatillos
My Favorite Vegetable Tacos with Tomatillos & Pico De Gallo 53

tomatoes
Jenny's Gypsy Soup 24
Kale Caesar with Cherry Tomato, Cucumber & Mock Parmesan 30
Liquid Prozac 79
My Favorite Vegetable Tacos with Tomatillos & Pico De Gallo 53
Quinoa & Fava Bean Chili 17
Red & Yellow Peppers Stuffed with Millet Salad 51

Red Quinoa, Fresh Corn, Blistered Tomatoes & Avocado 40
Roasted Balsamic Tofu with Gremolata & Cherry Tomatoes 60
Summer Marinara 54
Vegan "Chicken" Tortilla Soup 21
Winter Marinara 54

tortillas/tortilla chips
My Favorite Vegetable Tacos with Tomatillos & Pico De Gallo 53
Vegan "Chicken" Tortilla Soup 21

turnips
Braised Turnips with Miso 47

V

Vegan "Chicken" Tortilla Soup 21
Vegan Crispy Rice Treats 111
Vegan Quinoa & Lentil Burgers with Sriracha 64

veggies
Braised Turnips with Miso 47
Juicy Jenny Collard Wraps 52
My Favorite Vegetable Tacos with Tomatillos & Pico De Gallo 53
Red & Yellow Peppers Stuffed with Millet Salad 51
Roasted Rainbow 45
Roasted Sweet & Spicy Sweet Potatoes with Romesco Sauce 46
Spaghetti Squash with Summer or Winter Marinara 54
Zucchini Spaghetti with the Most Delicious Vegan Pesto 48

vinegar
Jenny's Every Day Dressing 120
Miso Dressing 120
Raw Collard, Apple, Sun Dried Figs & Candied Ginger with Apple Cider Vinaigrette 32
Roasted Balsamic Tofu with Gremolata & Cherry Tomatoes 60

W

Wake Up and Smell the Coffee Smoothie 94
walnuts
Raw Brownies 99
Raw Power Bar 106
watermelon
Superfuel 74
Wild Mushroom Potage 18
Winter Marinara 54

Y
Yummy Pumpkin Bread 113

Z
zucchini
Jenny's Gypsy Soup 24
My Favorite Vegetable Tacos with Tomatillos & Pico De Gallo 53
Quinoa & Fava Bean Chili 17
Raw Six Vegetable Spiralized Salad with Green Tahini Dressing 35
Zucchini Spaghetti with the Most Delicious Vegan Pesto 48
Zucchini Spaghetti with the Most Delicious Vegan Pesto 48

Jennifer Levison lives in Atlanta, Georgia with her son Jonah, two stray dogs and a crazy cat. When she's not traveling in search of her latest soup concoctions, she performs in local theaters and spends her time trying to inspire everyone on the planet to take better care of themselves and to be more present in their daily lives. Fortunately for her, there will never be a shortage of people who need inspiration.

If you've got a story, request, comment or question, please share it with us at souperjennyatl.com.